Woman's Duties in Social and Political Life

Political Life

BY

POPE PIUS XII

With Discussion Club Outline

BY REV. GERALD C. TREACY, S.J.

For Discussion Club Outline

Imprimi Potest:

JAMES P. SWEENEY, S.J.,
Provincial, Maryland-New York.

Woman's Duties in Social and Political Life

(Official N. C. W. C. Text)

1. Your presence in great numbers around Us, dear daughters, is especially significant at the present moment. For if We are always glad to receive you, bless you and give you Our paternal counsels, there is added circumstance now that, at your urgent request, We are to deal with a topic outstanding in interest and primary importance for our times: It is woman's duties in social and political life. We for Our part welcomed such an opportunity, for the feverish agitation of the present moment of travail, and still more apprehensions of an uncertain future, have brought the position of woman to the forefront in the programs of both friends and enemies of Christ and Church.

2. Let Us say at the outset that for Us the problem regarding woman, both in its entirety as a whole and in all its many details, resolves itself into preserving and augmenting that dignity which woman has from God. For Us, accordingly, it is not a problem that is merely juridical or economic, educational or biological, political or demographic—it is rather one which, in spite of its complexity, hinges entirely on the question how to maintain and strengthen that dignity of woman, especially today, in circumstances in which Providence has placed us.

3. To envisage the question any other way or to consider it exclusively under any of the aspects We just mentioned would be tantamount to shirking it without advantage to anyone, and least of all to woman herself. To detach it from God and from the order of things wisely set up by the Creator by His most holy will is to miss the essential point of the question, which is the dignity of woman, that dignity which she has only from God and in God.

4. Hence, it follows that those systems cannot treat the question of women's rights properly which exclude God and His law from the social life and give precepts of religion, at most, a lowly place in man's private life.

5. You, therefore, disregarding high-sounding and empty slogans with which some people would qualify the movement for women's rights, have laudably organized and united as Catholic women and Catholic girls in order to meet in a becoming manner the natural needs and true interests of your sex.

Characteristics of the Two Sexes and Their Mutual Co-ordination

6. What, then, is this dignity that a woman has from God? Put the question to human nature as formed by God and elevated and redeemed in the Blood of Christ.

7. In their personal dignity as children of God a man and woman are absolutely equal, as they are in relation to the last end of human life, which is everlasting union with God in the happiness of heaven. It is the undying glory of the Church that she put these truths in their proper light

and honorable place and that she has freed woman from degrading, unnatural slavery.

8. But a man and woman cannot maintain and perfect this equal dignity of theirs, unless by respecting and activating characteristic qualities which nature has given each of them, physical and spiritual qualities which cannot be eliminated, which cannot be reversed without nature itself stepping in to restore the balance. These characteristic qualities which divide the two sexes are so obvious to all that only willful blindness or a no less disastrous utopian doctrinaire attitude could overlook or practically ignore their significance in social relations.

9. The two sexes, by the very qualities that distinguish them, are mutually complementary to such an extent that their co-ordination makes itself felt in every phase of man's social life. We shall here recall only two of these phases because of their special importance: the married state and the state of celibacy embraced voluntarily in accordance with evangelical counsels.

The Married State

10. The result of a genuine marriage union involves more than children when God grants them to the married couple, and the material and spiritual advantages that accrue to mankind from family life. The whole civilized world, all its branches, peoples, and relations between peoples, even the Church itself—in a word, everything really good in mankind—benefits by the happy results when this family life is orderly and flourishing and when the young

are accustomed to look up to it, honor it and love it as a holy ideal.

11. But where the two sexes, forgetful of that intimate harmony willed and established by God, give themselves up to perverted individualism, where their mutual relations are governed by selfishness and covetousness, when they do not collaborate by mutual accord for the service of mankind according to the designs of God and nature, when the young, scouting their responsibilities, silly and frivolous in spirit and conduct, render themselves unfit physically and morally for the holy state of Matrimony: then the common good of human society, in the temporal as well as the spiritual order, is gravely compromised and the Church of God herself trembles, not for her existence—for she has divine promises —but for the large achievements of her mission to men.

Voluntary Celibacy According to Evangelical Counsels

12. But let us remember that for nigh on to twenty centuries, in every generation, thousands and thousands of men and women, from among the best, in order to follow the counsels of Christ, freely renounced the possibility of a family of their own and the sacred duties and rights of married life.

13. Is the common good of the peoples and the Church perhaps jeapardized by this? On the contrary, these generous souls recognize the union of the two sexes in Matrimony as a good of high order. But, if they abandon the ordinary way and leave the beaten track, they do not desert

it, but rather consecrate themselves to the service of mankind with a complete disregard for themselves and their own interests by an act incomparably broader in its scope, more all-embracing and universal.

14. Look at those men and women: see them dedicated to prayer and penance, intent on the instruction and education of the young and ignorant, leaning over the pillow of the sick and dying, open-hearted for all their miseries, and all their weaknesses in order to relieve them, ease them, lighten them and sanctify them.

The Catholic Girl Who Remains Perforce Unmarried

15. When one thinks of young girls and women who willingly renounce Matrimony in order to consecrate themselves to a higher life of contemplation, sacrifice and charity, there comes at once to the lips the word that explains it: vocation. It is the only word that can describe so lofty a sentiment.

16. This vocation call of life is felt in the most diverse ways, corresponding to the infinitely diverse modulations of the voice of God; it may be an overpowering call, affectionately inviting inspiration, or gentle impulse—but the young Catholic girl, too, who remains unmarried perforce, trusting nonetheless the providence of our Heavenly Father, recognizes in the vicissitudes of life the call of the Master: The Master is come and calleth for thee (John xi. 28). She hearkens. She gives up the fond dream of her adolescence and youth to have a faithful companion in life and set up a family. And in the exclusion of Matrimony she recognizes

her vocation. Then, with a sorrowful but submissive heart, she, too, gives herself up to the noble and most diversified good works.

Motherhood the Natural Sphere of Woman

17. In both states alike woman's sphere is clearly outlined by qualities, temperament and gifts peculiar to her sex. She collaborates with man but in a manner proper to her according to her natural bent. Now the sphere of woman, her manner of life, her native bent, is motherhood. Every woman is made to be a mother: a mother in the physical meaning of the word or in the more spiritual and exalted but no less real sense.

18. For this purpose the Creator organized the whole characteristic make-up of woman, her organic construction, but even more her spirit, and above all her delicate sensitiveness. Thus it is that a woman who is a real woman can see all the problems of human life only in the perspective of the family. That is why her delicate sense of her dignity puts her on guard any time that a social or political order threatens to prejudice her mission as a mother or the good of the family.

19. And such, unfortunately, is the social and political situation today; it might even become still more precarious for the sanctity of the home and hence for woman's dignity. Your day is here, Catholic women and girls. Public life needs you. To each one of you might be said: (tua res agitur) your destiny is at stake. (Horace Epistles 1-18-84.)

Social and Political Situation Unfavorable to Sanctity of the Family and Woman's Dignity

20. It is beyond dispute that for a long time past the political situation has been evolving in a manner unfavorable to the real welfare of the family and women. Many political movements are turning to woman to win her for their cause. Some totalitarian systems dangle marvelous promises before her eyes: equality of rights with men, care during pregnancy and childbirth; public kitchens and other communal services to free her from some of her household cares, public kindergartens and other institutions maintained and administered by government which relieve her of maternal obligations towards her own children, free schools and sick benefits.

21. It is not meant to deny the advantages that can accrue from one and the other of these social services if properly administered. Indeed, We have on a former occasion pointed out that for the same work output a woman is entitled to the same wages as a man. But there still remains the crucial point of the question to which We already referred. Has woman's position been thereby improved?

22. Equality of rights with man brought with it her abandonment of the home where she reigned as queen, and her subjection to the same work strain and working hours. It entails depreciation of her true dignity and the solid foundation of all her rights which is her characteristic feminine role, and the intimate co-ordination of the two sexes. The end intended by God for the good of all human society, especially for that of the family, is lost sight of. In conces-

sions made to woman one can easily see not respect for her dignity or her mission, but an attempt to foster the economic and military power of the totalitarian state to which all must inexorably be subordinated.

23. On the other hand, can a woman, perhaps, hope for her real well-being from a regime dominated by capitalism? We do not need to describe to you now the economic and social results that issue from it. You know its characteristic signs, and you yourselves are bearing its burden; excessive concentration of populations in cities, the constant all-absorbing increase of big industries, the difficult and precarious state of others, notably those of artisan and agricultural workers and the disturbing increase of unemployment.

24. To restore as far as possible the honor of the woman's and mother's place in the home: that is the watchword one hears now from many quarters like a cry of alarm, as if the world was awakening, terrified by the fruits of material and scientific progress of which it before was so proud.

Let us look at things as they are:

Woman's Absence from the Home

25. We see a woman who in order to augment her husband's earnings, betakes herself also to a factory, leaving her house abandoned during her absence. The house, untidy and small perhaps before, becomes even more miserable for lack of care. Members of the family work separately in four quarters of the city and with different working hours. Scarcely ever do they find themselves together

for dinner or rest after work—still less for prayer in common. What is left of family life? And what attractions can it offer to children?

Malformation in Education of Young Girls

26. To such painful consequences of the absence of the mother from the home there is added another, still more deplorable. It concerns the education, especially of the young girl, and her preparation for real life. Accustomed as she is to see her mother always out of the house and the house itself so gloomy in its abandonment, she will be unable to find any attraction for it, she will not feel the slightest inclination for austere housekeeping jobs. She cannot be expected to appreciate their nobility and beauty or to wish one day to give herself to them as a wife and mother.

27. This is true in all grades and stations of social life. The daughter of the worldly woman, who sees all housekeeping left in the hands of paid help and her mother fussing around with frivolous occupations and futile amusements, will follow her example, will want to be emancipated as soon as possible and in the words of a very tragic phrase "to live her own life." How could she conceive a desire to become one day a true lady that is the mother of a happy, prosperous, worthy family?

28. As to the working classes, forced to earn daily bread a woman might, if she reflected, realize that not rarely the supplementary wage which she earns by working outside the house is easily swallowed up by other expenses or even by waste which is ruinous to the family budget. The daughter

who also goes out to work in a factory or office, deafened by the excited restless world in which she lives, dazzled by the tinsel of specious luxury, developing a thirst for shallow pleasures that distract but do not give satiety or repose in those revue or dance halls which are sprouting up everywhere, often for party propaganda purposes, and which corrupt youth, becomes a fashionable lady, and despises the old nineteenth century ways of life.

29. How could she not feel her modest home surroundings unattractive and more squalid than they are in reality? To find her pleasure in them, to desire one day to settle in them herself, she should be able to offset her natural impressions by a serious intellectual and spiritual life, by the vigor that comes from religious education and from supernatural ideals. But what kind of religious formation has she received in such surroundings?

30. And that is not all. When, as the years pass, her mother prematurely aged, worn out, and broken by work beyond her capacity, by sorrow and anxiety, will see her return home at night at a very late hour, she will not find her a support or a help but rather the mother herself will have to wait on a daughter incapable and unaccustomed to household work and to perform for her all the offices of a servant.

31. And the lot of the father will not be any better when old age, sickness, infirmity and unemployment force him to depend for his meager sustenance on the good or bad will of his children. Here you have the august holy authority of the father and mother dethroned.

The Duty of a Woman to Take Part in Public Life at the Present Time

32. Shall we conclude then that you Catholic women and girls must show yourselves adverse to a movement which willy-nilly carried you with it in social and political life? Certainly not.

33. In the face of theories and practice which by different ways are tearing a woman from her mission and, with a flattering promise of unbridled freedom or, in reality, of hopeless misery, are depriving her of her personal dignity, her dignity as woman, We have heard the cry of fear which calls for her active presence as far as possible in the home.

34. A woman is, in fact, kept out of the home not only by her so-called emancipation but often, too, by the necessities of life, by the continuous anxiety about daily bread. It would be useless then to preach to her to return to the home while conditions prevail which constrain her to remain away from it. And this brings Us to the first aspect of your mission in the social and political life which opens up before you.

35. Your entry into public life came about suddenly as a result of social upheavals which we see around us. It does not matter. You are called upon to take part. Will you, perhaps, leave to others, to those who sponsor or collaborate in the ruin of some monopoly of social organization of which the family is the primary factor in its economic, juridical, spiritual and moral unity?

36. The fate of the family, the fate of human relations are at stake. They are in your hands (tua res agitur). Every woman has then, mark it well, the obligation, the strict obligation in conscience, not to absent herself but to go into action in a manner and way suitable to the condition of each so as to hold back those currents which threaten the home, so as to oppose those doctrines which undermine its foundations, so as to prepare, organize and achieve its restoration.

37. To this powerful motive which impels a Catholic woman to enter upon a way that now is opened to her activity, there is added another, her dignity as a woman. She has to collaborate with man towards the good of the State in which she is of the same dignity as he. Each of the two sexes must take the part that belongs to it, according to its nature, special qualities, and physical, intellectual and moral aptitude. Both have the right and duty to co-operate toward the total good of society and of their country.

38. But it is clear that if man is by temperament more drawn to deal with external things and public affairs, woman has, generally speaking, more perspicacity and a finer touch in knowing and solving delicate problems of domestic and family life which is the foundation of all social life. This does not exclude the possibility of some women giving genuine proof of great talent in all fields of public activity.

39. All this is a question, not so much of distinct assignments, as of the manner of judging and coming to concrete practical conclusions. Let us take the case of civil rights: These are at present the same for both, but with how much

more discernment and efficacy will they be utilized if man and woman come to complement one another. The sensitiveness and fine feeling proper to woman, which might lead her to judge by her impressions and would thus involve the risk of impeding clarity and breadth of vision, serenity of judgment and forethought for remote consequences, are, on the contrary, of immense help when it is a question of throwing light on the needs, aspirations and dangers that touch domestic, public welfare or religious spheres.

The Vast Field of Activity for Woman in Present-Day Civil and Political Life

40. Woman's activity is concerned, in great part, with the labors and occupations of domestic life which contribute to a greater and more beneficial extent than generally is thought to the true interests of social relations. But these interests also call for a group of women who can dispose of more time so as to devote themselves to them more directly and more entirely.

41. Who, then, can these women be, if not especially (we certainly do not mean exclusively) those whom we referred to a little while ago, those on whom unavoidable circumstances bestowed a mysterious vocation, whom events destined to a solitude which was not in their thoughts or desires, and which seemed to condemn them to a selfishly futile and aimless life?

42. Today, on the contrary, their mission is unfolded—multifarious, militant, calling for all their energies and of such a nature that few others held down by cares of family

or education of children, or subject to the holy yoke of rule have equal opportunities of fulfilling it.

43. Up to now, some of those women dedicated their lives with a zeal often wonderful to parochial works, others with even larger views consecrated themselves to moral and social activity of great consequence. Their numbers as a result of the war and the calamities which followed it are considerably increased. Many brave men have fallen in the dreadful war, others returned invalids. Many young women will, therefore, wait in vain for the return of a husband and the flowering of new lives in their solitary home. But, at the same time, new needs created by the entry of woman into civil and political life have arisen to claim their assistance. Is it just a strange coincidence or are we to see in it the disposition of Divine Providence?

44. Thus it is a vast field of activity which now lies open to woman and it can be corresponding to the mentality of character of each, either intellectual or actively practical To study and expound the place and role of woman in society, her rights and duties; to become a teacher-guide to one's sisters and to direct ideas, dissipate prejudices, clarify obscure points, explain and diffuse the teachings of the Church in order more securely to discredit error, illusion and falsehood, in order to expose more effectively the tactics of those who oppose Catholic dogma and morals—is an immense work and one of impelling necessity, without which all the zeal of the Apostolate could obtain but precarious results. But direct action, too, is indispensable if we do not want the same doctrines and solid convictions to remain, if

not entirely of academic interest, at least of little practical consequences.

45. This direct participation, this effective collaboration in social and political activity does not at all change the normal activity of woman. Associated with men in civil institutions, she will apply herself especially to those matters which call for tact, delicacy and maternal instinct rather than administrative rigidity. Who better than she can understand what is needed for the dignity of woman, the integrity and honor of the young girl, and the protection and education of the child?

46. And in all these question, how many problems call for study and action on the part of governments and legislators. Only a woman will know, for instance, how to temper with kindness, without detriment to its efficacy, legislation to repress licentiousness. She alone can find the means to save from degradation and to raise in honesty and in religious and civil virtues the morally derelict young. She alone will be able to render effective the work of protection and rehabilitation for those freed from prison and for fallen girls. She alone will re-echo from her own heart the plea of mothers from whom the totalitarian state, by whatever name it be called, would will to snatch the education of their children.

Some Considerations in Conclusion

47. (A) On the preparation and formation of woman for social and political life.

48. We outlined a program of woman's duties. Its practical aim is twofold—her preparation and formation for social and political life, and the evolution and activation of this social and political life in private and in public.

49. It is clear that woman's task thus understood cannot be improvised. Motherly instinct is in her a human instinct, not determined by nature down to the details of its application. It is directed by free will and this in turn is guided by intellect. Hence comes its moral value and its dignity but also imperfection which must be compensated for and redeemed by education.

50. Education proper to her sex of the young girl, and not rarely also of the grown woman, is therefore a necessary condition of her preparation and formation for a life worthy of her. The ideal would evidently be that this education should begin with infancy in the intimacy of the Catholic home under the directions of the mother. It is, unfortunately, not always the case, not always possible.

51. However, it is possible to supply, at least in part, for this deficiency by securing for the young girl who of necessity must work outside the home one of those occupations which are, to some extent, a training ground and a noviceship for the life for which she is destined. To such a purpose also serve those schools of domestic economy which aim at making of the child and the young girl of today the wife and mother of tomorrow.

52. How worthy of praise and encouragement are such institutions! They are one of the forms of activity in which your motherly sense and zeal can have ample scope and

influence and one, too, of the most precious because the good that you do propagates itself to infinity, preparing your pupils to pass on to others in the family, or out of it, the good which you have done them. What should we say, besides, of many other kindly offices by which you come to the aid of mothers of families in what concerns their intellectual and religious formation and in the sad and difficult circumstances in which their life moves?

53. (B) On the practical activation of woman's social and political life.

54. But in your social and political activity much depends on the legislation of the State and the administration of local bodies. Accordingly, the electoral ballot in the hands of Catholic women is an important means toward the fulfillment of their strict duty in conscience, especially at the present time. The State and politics have, in fact, precisely the office of securing for the family of every social class conditions necessary for them to exist and to evolve as economic, juridical, and moral units. Then the family will really be the vital nucleus of men who are earning honestly their temporal and eternal welfare.

55. All this, of course, the real woman easily understands. But what she does not, and cannot, understand, is that by politics is meant domination by one class of others, and the ambitious striving for ever more extensive economic and national empire—or whatever pretended motive such ambition be based. For she knows that such a policy paves the way to hidden or open civil war, to the ever-growing

accumulation of armaments and to the constant danger of war.

56. She knows from experience that in any event this policy is harmful to the family which must pay for it at a high price in goods and blood. Accordingly, no wise woman favors a policy of class struggle or war. Her vote is a vote for peace. Hence, in the interest and for the good of the family she will hold to that norm, and she will always refuse her vote to any tendency, from whatever quarter it hails, to the selfish desires of domination, internal or external, of the peace of the nation.

57. Courage then, Catholic women and girls! Work without ceasing, without allowing yourselves ever to be discouraged by difficulties or obstacles. May you be—under the standard of Christ the King, under the patronage of His wonderful Mother—restorers of home, family and society.

58. May Divine favors descend on you in a copious stream: Favors in token of which We impart to you with all the affection of Our paternal heart an Apostolic Benediction.

DISCUSSION CLUB OUTLINE

Prepared by GERALD C. TREACY, *S.J.*

Numerals Indicate Paragraphs

LESSON I

Paragraphs 1 to 11

WOMAN'S DUTIES IN SOCIAL AND POLITICAL LIFE

The present crisis in world affairs has brought woman's position to the forefront in the programs of both friends and enemies of Christ and His Church. We welcome then the opportunity to discuss woman's duties in social and political life.

THE DIGNITY OF WOMAN

Woman's dignity is from God. It is Our task to preserve and increase that dignity. The educational, economic and political position of modern woman hinge on one thing alone—woman's dignity. It is Our duty to maintain and strengthen that dignity, especially today when the world is passing through a momentous crisis. To view woman's position merely from an economic, political, or educational angle, would be to shirk the real point at issue, which is woman's dignity. It would do no good to anyone, least of all woman herself.

Woman's dignity comes from God and rests in God. Hence no system advocating woman's rights can benefit woman unless its teaching is rooted in this basic principle.

THE CHARACTERISTICS OF THE TWO SEXES

Man and woman are completely equal in their personal dignity as children of God, as they are in their common destiny which is everlasting union with God in the happiness of heaven. The Church by proclaiming this truth through all the centuries of her history, has freed woman from the degrading, unnatural slavery that was her lot under Paganism.

Man and woman, while equal, are different. So to maintain and perfect this equal dignity, man and woman must respect and promote the individual characteristic qualities which Nature has conferred on each of them. These qualities are both physical and spiritual. These qualities can neither be ignored nor destroyed. Those characteristic qualities which differentiate the sexes are obvious to everyone. They cannot be overlooked in social relations.

These differentiating qualities make the sexes complementary. Their co-ordination makes itself felt in every phase of man's social life. Here we wish to mention two phases of man's social life, the married state and the state of celibacy, voluntarily embraced according to the Evangelical Counsels.

THE MARRIED STATE

Marriage is the foundation of society. Church and State rest upon it. As the family goes so goes civilization. When man and woman forget this and allow selfish individualism to prevail in their marital relationship, then Church and State suffer irreparable harm. Marriage is from God and not from man's whims. And young people who render themselves unfit physically and morally for the holy vocation of matrimony, outrage God's sacred law and destroy the very bulwark of civilization.

QUESTIONS

What was the occasion of the present address?

What is the topic treated?

What does the problem regarding woman resolve itself into?

Is the problem political, economic or educational?

Express the problem in a few words.

What foundation is the basis of woman's rights?

Explain how man and woman are completely equal.

Who has ever proclaimed this equality?

How is the equal dignity of man and woman to be perfected?

What characteristics must ever be considered in all social relationships?

What does the result of a true marriage union involve?

Everything really good in the world of men depends on what?

What condition threatens the common good of society and the Church?

LESSON II

Paragraphs 12 to 19

VOLUNTARY CELIBACY

In every century of the history of the Church, and in every generation thousands of men and women have renounced the rights of marriage, sacrificed the joys of motherhood and fatherhood and dedicated themselves to a celibate life, following Christ's Counsels. Does this harm the common good of the Church and society? By no means. These generous souls give up matrimony, not because they be-little its sacredness but because they wish to serve the whole human family in a life of prayer, penance and un-stinted service of their fellow men, in closer imitation of the God-Man. When one thinks of young girls with all human happiness before them, passing it by for a life of sacrifice, there is only one explanation and that is VOCA-TION.

THE MEANING OF VOCATION

Vocation is God's call to a life especially consecrated to Him. It comes in diverse ways, as diverse as the Grace of God. It urges some girls to follow the religious life. It urges others to sacrifice the rights and happiness of mar-riage in order to lead a life more completely dedicated to good works, outside the religious life.

MOTHERHOOD WOMAN'S SPHERE

In both the married and unmarried state woman's sphere is clearly outlined by qualities, temperament and gifts be-longing exclusively to her sex. She collaborates with man according to her natural bent. Her natural bent is mother-hood. Every woman is made to be a mother, in the phys-ical sense or in the more spiritual but no less real sense. This is proved by the whole characteristic make-up of woman, her organic structure, her spirit, her delicate sen-sitiveness. That is why the real woman views all life's problems in the perspective of the family. That is why her delicate sense ever puts her on guard against any social or political movement that threatens her mission as a mother or the welfare of the family. Unfortunately this is the MODERN THREAT, in today's social and political situation. Catholic women and girls YOUR DAY is here. PUBLIC LIFE needs you. YOUR DESTINY is at stake.

QUESTIONS

Is the common good of society and the Church hurt by the celibates?

What is the purpose of those leading the celibate life?

How do they spend their lives?

How explain the young girls' sacrifice in entering religious life?

Is the vocation to the religious life the only vocation?

Every woman is made to be a mother. Explain.

How may God's purpose in creating woman be recognized?

In what perspective does a true woman see life's problems?

The Pope tells women and girls: "Your day is here." Explain.

LESSON III

Paragraphs 20 to 31

TRENDS UNFAVORABLE TO WOMAN'S DIGNITY

Recent political trends have been developing in a manner unfavorable to woman's real welfare and the good of the family. One example is totalitarianism. It has dangled fair promises before woman, eager to gain her support. Many totalitarian regimes have offered her equal rights with men, and many social services to relieve her of burdensome home duties. We do not question the value of these services, if properly administered. Indeed We maintain and have always maintained that for the same work a woman is entitled to the same wages as a man. The real point however is this: has woman's position been thereby improved?

Equality of rights has induced woman to abandon the home where she once reigned as queen. She has been subjected to the same work strain as men. God's end for woman as wife and mother has been ignored; the foundation of her true dignity which rests on her peculiar feminine role has been belittled. In concessions granted woman by totalitarianism may be seen not any regard for her dignity and mission, but an attempt to foster the economic and military power of the totalitarian State upon men and women inexorably.

The same holds true for a regime dominated by unbridled capitalism. Money and the making of money being the gospel of such a regime, you are familiar with its results; overpopulated cities, constantly increasing big industries with disturbing increase of unemployment. In the face of these bitter results We now on all sides hear the cry of alarm: "Restore woman to her place in the home as wife and mother."

THE HOME WITH WOMAN ABSENT

What picture does the home present in which the mother is at work? Unkempt and untidy it is nothing more than a shelter in which there is no family spirit, no common family life, and no common family prayers. For children the street is more attractive than such a home.

NEGLECTED EDUCATION OF GIRLS

The education of girls in such a home is neglected. Seeing the mother shirk all household duties, the girl will grow to despise all the worthy tasks of a good housewife. She will have but one desire, to escape as soon as possible from such a home and lead her own life.

In workers' families often the wages earned by the absent mother and daughters are squandered. The young girl worker absorbed by the excitement of the world into which she has been thrown, grows to crave luxury and to look down upon the career of the woman in the home. What intellectual or spiritual formation can a girl receive from such a neglected home? And as the years pass and mother and father are both unfitted for work, what help are they to hope for from such a daughter?

QUESTIONS

How has the recent political situation been affecting woman and the family?

How has totalitarianism attracted woman?

What may be said of the social services offered by totalitarianism?

What is the Pope's stand on woman's wages?

What is the crucial question pertaining to woman?

What did equality of rights bring with it?

What was the aim of totalitarianism in offering benefits to woman?

What have been the results of unbridled capitalism?

What is the cry of alarm now being shouted?

Enumerate the effects on home life when the mother goes out to work.

How does the absence of the mother affect a girl's home education?

What often happens to the extra wages earned by the woman worker?

LESSON IV

Paragraphs 32 to 39

WOMAN'S DUTY IN PUBLIC LIFE

Despite the fact that woman's supreme place is the home, modern conditions call for woman's participation in public life, social and political. It is a duty in conscience for the Catholic woman to take an active part in the political and social movements of the day, and not to abandon the field to those who are striking at the very foundation of the home. Catholic women, the fate of human relations, the fate of the family are at stake. They are in your hands. You must collaborate with men for the good of the State for you have the same dignity as men. You have the right and duty to co-operate with men for the total good of society and your country. Woman has a contribution to make to the commonweal by her influence in public life that she alone by her nature is capable of making, especially in matters touching domestic and religious spheres.

QUESTIONS

Under present conditions is woman free to remain at home?

What accounts for the entrance of woman into public life?

What is the strict obligation of every Catholic woman today?

What policy must be followed by man and woman in exercising their civil rights?

In whose hands rests the fate of human relations and the family?

LESSON V

Paragraphs 40 to 46

THE MODERN APOSTOLATE OF WOMEN

Woman's concern is primarily with domestic life. For that very reason she is fitted to take an active part in safeguarding that life by political and social action. And who are better able to enter this field than those whose vocation it is to remain unmarried while dedicating themselves to good works. This is truly their day for real Catholic Action, unhampered as they are by the cares of a family or by the necessary restriction of a religious rule. New needs call for their help. A vast field of activity now lies open to woman. Knowing the rights and duties of woman, the Catholic woman is capable of spreading the teaching of her Church, and so to stem the tide of modern error, that under the name of emancipation really works for the degradation of woman.

Direct Action Needed

Direct political and social action is called for. But that must be womanly action. Associated with men in civil office, woman will wield her influence in those matters that belong especially to woman's welfare. Her maternal instinct will speak in securing legislation that is for the benefit of the family. She better than man will safeguard the dignity of her own sex. She will be more alert to the dangers of totalitarianism, by whatever name it may be called.

QUESTIONS

Who among women are especially called to the modern woman's apostolate?

Why is this type of woman especially fitted?

Are we to see in this a design of Divine Providence? What does that mean?

How should woman meet this vast opportunity now open to her?

Why is direct action indispensable?

Will this change the normal activity of woman?

To what matters will she especially apply her abilities?

What field is woman eminently qualified to cover?

What is the twofold practical aim of woman's apostolate?

LESSON VI
Paragraphs 47 to 58

The Education of Woman for Public Life

To fill her place in Public Life woman needs education.

30

That education must begin in the home, and be continued by the school. Schools for training young girls in domestic science are of great value, as they are preparing the wives and mothers of tomorrow.

WOMAN AND THE BALLOT

As so much depends today on sound legislation, the choice of worthy legislators is of supreme importance. The proper use of the ballot is a duty in conscience for the Catholic woman. Good social legislation is the duty of the State, that every family may develop and prosper, to whatever class in society it may belong. For the family is the most important unit in the State. Who is better aware of that than woman? And the real woman understands this clearly.

REAL POLITICS

And the real woman understands too that real politics, that is the activity of the State and government must be bent on the common welfare, the good of the family and its individual members. And she will not admit that politics means the domination of one class, or economic or national imperialism. For she knows that such is the pathway to war.

She knows well that such politics harm the family, which has to pay the price in suffering and blood. So no real woman favors class conflict or war. Her vote is always for peace. And her vote is always against any policy that tends to threaten the peace of the nation. May woman under the standard of Christ the King and under the patronage of His wonderful Mother be the restorer of home, family and society.

QUESTIONS

What does the Pope say on the need of woman's education?

What is the value of schools of domestic science?

How should woman properly influence legislation?

What is the office of the State and politics according to the Pope?

What is the inevitable consequence of class domination and imperialism?

How will woman's vote always be cast?

What are Pope Pius' final words?

Made in the USA
Lexington, KY
04 December 2014